Scary Creatures
PINNIPEDS

Written by
John Malam

Created and designed
by David Salariya

BOOK HOUSE

Author:

John Malam studied ancient history and archaeology at the University of Birmingham, England, after which he worked as an archaeologist at the Ironbridge Gorge Museum in Shropshire. He is now an author specialising in information books for children on a wide range of subjects. He lives in Cheshire with his wife and their two young children. Website: www.johnmalam.co.uk

Artists:

Janet Baker and Julian Baker
 (JB Illustrations)
Robert Morton
Carolyn Franklin
Mark Bergin

Series Creator:

David Salariya was born in Dundee, Scotland. In 1989 he established The Salariya Book Company. He has illustrated a wide range of books and has created many new series for publishers in the UK and overseas. He lives in Brighton with his wife, illustrator Shirley Willis, and their son.

Editor: Tanya Kant

Editorial Assistant:
Rob Walker

Picture Research:
Mark Bergin, Carolyn Franklin

Photo Credits:

Dreamstime: 11, 15, 25, 29
Fotolia: 19, 24
iStockphoto: 9, 12, 16, 17, 18, 20–21, 22, 23, 26, 28

Trained sea lion

Published in Great Britain in MMIX by
Book House, an imprint of
The Salariya Book Company Ltd
25 Marlborough Place, Brighton BN1 1UB

SALARIYA

A catalogue record for this book is available from the British Library.

HB ISBN: 978-1-906714-05-5
PB ISBN: 978-1-906714-06-2

Printed in China

Visit our website at **www.book-house.co.uk**
or go to **www.salariya.com** for *free* electronic versions of:
You Wouldn't Want to be an Egyptian Mummy!
You Wouldn't Want to be a Roman Gladiator!
Avoid Joining Shackleton's Polar Expedition!
Avoid Sailing on a 19th-Century Whaling Ship!

PAPER FROM
SUSTAINABLE
FORESTS

Contents

What are pinnipeds? 4

How does a pinniped swim? 6

What's inside a pinniped? 9

What do pinnipeds eat? 10

How deep can pinnipeds dive? 12

Who preys on pinnipeds? 15

What is the life cycle of a pinniped? 16

Why do pinnipeds shed their fur? 18

How far do pinnipeds travel? 20

Why do pinnipeds sing? 22

Are pinnipeds in danger? 24

How are pinnipeds used by humans? 26

Pinnipeds around the world 28

Pinniped facts 30

Glossary 31

Index 32

Walrus

What are pinnipeds?

Pinnipeds are **mammals** that live in the sea, in freshwater, and on land and ice. They live in the icy Arctic and Antarctic oceans, and in warmer waters around the world. There are three families of pinnipeds: seals, sea lions and walruses. 'Pinniped' means 'fin-footed', which gives us a clue to how these animals move. When they are on land or ice, they use their fins, or flippers, to move around.

There are thirty-three different **species** of seals, sea lions and walruses.

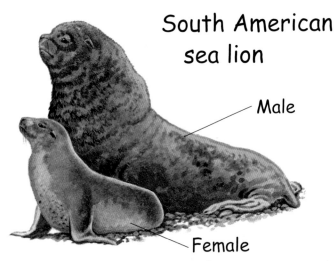

South American sea lion

— Male

— Female

What is a sea lion?

A sea lion is a pinniped known as an **otariid**. An otariid is called an eared seal because it has tiny ear flaps on the outside of its body. Their hind (back) flippers are hairless. An otariid can turn these flippers forward and walk on them like feet.

Leopard seal

What is a seal?

A seal is a pinniped known as a **phocid**. A phocid is also called a true seal or earless seal. It does not have ear flaps on the outside of its body. Instead, it has tiny ear holes. Its hind flippers are furry and cannot be folded underneath its body to be used as feet.

Did You Know?

The body of a sea lion is so flexible that it can bend over backwards and almost touch the tips of its hind flippers with its front flippers.

Southern elephant seal (phocid)

Male

Female

Northern fur seal (otariid)

Male

Female

Pacific walrus

Tusks

What is a walrus?

A walrus is a pinniped known as an **odobenid**. An odobenid seal is an earless seal, like a phocid seal. It has hairless hind flippers that work as feet on land, like an otariid seal. Its upper **canine teeth** have developed into two long tusks.

How big are pinnipeds?

Pinniped species grow to different sizes. The shortest pinniped is the Baikal seal, which is found only in Lake Baikal, Russia. They grow to about 1.4 metres long. The longest and heaviest pinniped is the southern elephant seal, which grows to 5 metres and can weigh up to 4.5 tonnes.

How does a pinniped swim?

Pinnipeds have rounded, smooth bodies that move quickly through water. Pinnipeds can swim fast over short distances, but most of the time they swim at a steady cruising speed.

X-Ray Vision

Hold the next page up to the light to see what's inside a leopard seal.

See what's inside

Seals and walruses swim by moving their hind flippers from side to side. They use their fore (front) flippers for steering. Sea lions, however, use their fore flippers for moving and their hind flippers for steering.

Hind flippers

Leopard seal

Fore flippers

Pinnipeds are rounded because under their skin there is a thick layer of fat called **blubber**. It keeps them warm and allows them to live in cold places.

Leopard seal

Streamlined body

Thick,
short fur

Hind flipper

Short,
thick neck

Fore flipper

Short whiskers

Chinstrap penguin

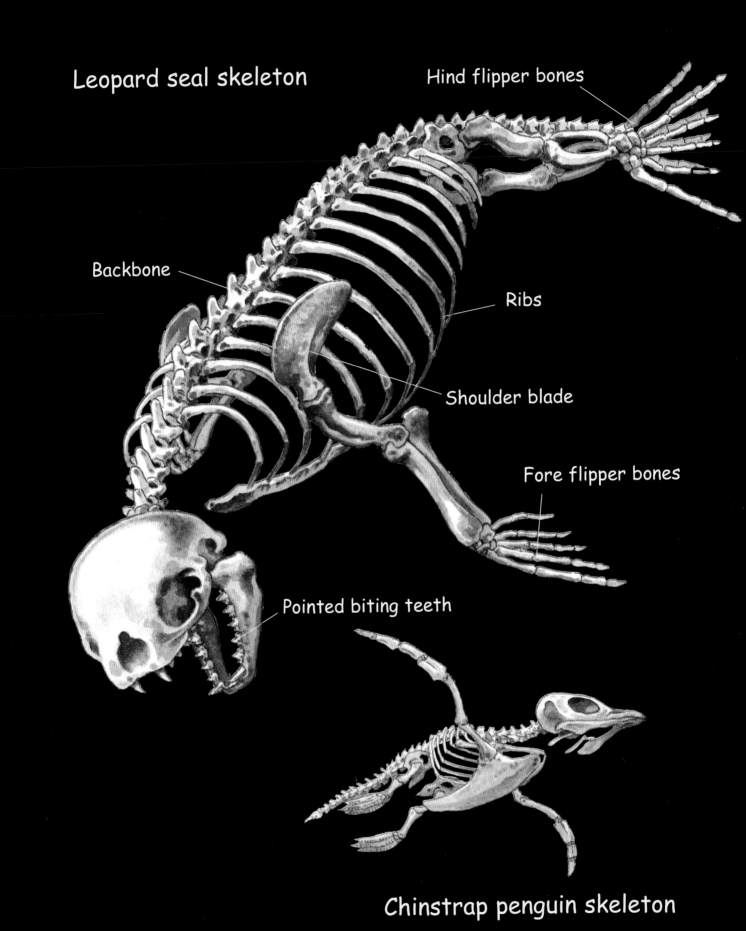

Leopard seal skeleton

Hind flipper bones

Backbone

Ribs

Shoulder blade

Fore flipper bones

Pointed biting teeth

Chinstrap penguin skeleton

What's inside a pinniped?

All pinnipeds have a flexible skeleton inside their bodies. Seals and sea lions have pointed teeth that are designed for catching and holding on to slippery **prey**, especially fish and squid. Walruses have front teeth that have grown into tusks.

Why do walruses have tusks?

Walruses use their tusks to pull themselves out of the water and onto the ice. During the breeding season, male walruses display their tusks to attract females. Males' tusks are longer and heavier than those of females.

Why do pinnipeds swallow stones?

Gastroliths

Many pinnipeds swallow small stones. These stones, known as **gastroliths**, stay in their stomachs. Scientists think these stones might help to digest food by crushing it, or they might help pinnipeds keep their balance underwater.

Adult walruses displaying their tusks to each other

What do pinnipeds eat?

Pinnipeds are **carnivores** (meat-eaters). They mostly eat small sea animals, especially fish, shrimp, **krill**, octopus and squid. Leopard seals will eat larger animals, such as penguins and other pinnipeds. Walruses prefer to eat animals that live on the seabed, such as clams, crabs and sea cucumbers.

Leopard seals catch penguins either by chasing them underwater, or by breaking through thin ice and snatching them from below. The seal tosses the penguin around, beating it against the water until it is dead and its skin comes off. Then the seal eats the body. It doesn't eat the feathers, skin, feet or beak.

Pinniped prey

How does a walrus eat a clam?

First, the walrus finds the clam by stirring up mud on the seabed, either with its flippers or by squirting water out of its mouth. Then it sucks the clam from its shell, or blasts it out with a jet of water. A walrus can find and eat six clams a minute!

Adélie penguin

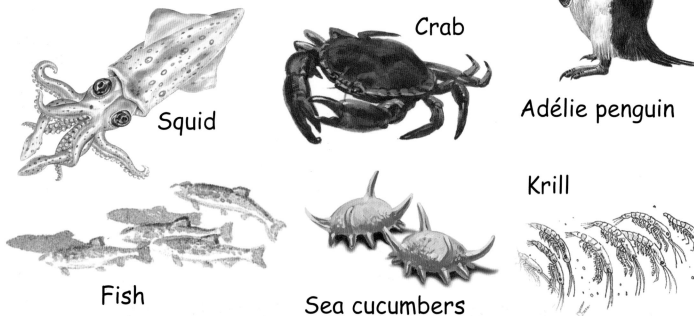

Crab

Squid

Krill

Fish

Sea cucumbers

Did You Know?

In 1967, four leopard seals killed 15,000 penguins on Ross Island, Antarctica, in 15 weeks. One seal ate six penguins in 1 hour and 10 minutes.

This sea lion has just caught a fish.

The sea lion eats the fish's body but leaves the head and tail.

How deep can pinnipeds dive?

Pinnipeds can dive to great depths and can stay underwater for a long time. Elephant seals dive the deepest, down to 1,250 metres. Walruses are shallow divers and rarely go deeper than 80 metres.

How long can a pinniped hold its breath?

A walrus can hold its breath for about 10 minutes, and a sea lion for about 20 minutes. A Weddell seal can stay under the water for 70 minutes before returning to the surface for air. A southern elephant seal can stay submerged for up to 2 hours.

X-Ray Vision

Hold the next page up to the light to see what's about to grab a seal.

See what happens

A walrus swimming underwater

Young elephant seal

Female elephant seal

Male elephant seal

Killer whale

Young seal

14

Who preys on pinnipeds?

Pinnipeds have many **predators**. On land and ice, pinnipeds are attacked for their meat by polar bears, wolves, eagles, pumas and brown hyenas. Humans also hunt them for their fur, blubber and meat. At sea, pinnipeds are hunted by sharks and killer whales. Pinnipeds also attack and eat other pinnipeds.

Out at sea, killer whales herd seals together, then swim through the group to grab individuals. They also snatch seals from the shore, almost **beaching** themselves as they lunge at the surprised seals.

Did You Know?

Polar bears have been seen throwing chunks of ice at walruses and seals, perhaps to stun them before moving in for the kill.

In the Arctic, polar bears hunt seals, especially ringed seals.

What is the life cycle of a pinniped?

Pinniped mothers carry their babies inside them for about eleven months. Babies, called **pups**, are born on land or ice. Pups feed on their mother's fat-rich milk and quickly gain weight. After they are **weaned**, the pups leave their mothers. The pups will start their own families when they are around four years old.

Pinnipeds live for about 15 to 25 years. Female pinnipeds (called **cows**) live longer than males (called **bulls**). It's thought that wild pinnipeds live longer than those in zoos.

Galápagos sea lion mother feeding her pup with milk

Large **colony** of Cape fur seals in Namibia, southern Africa

Some pinnipeds are solitary animals and live on their own; these include Ross seals, Baikal seals and crabeater seals. Others, such as elephant seals, sea lions and walruses, live in groups. During the breeding season, some seals come ashore in large numbers to form colonies or **rookeries** – places where pinnipeds breed and raise their young together.

Why do pinnipeds shed their fur?

Most pinnipeds have thick fur that helps to keep them warm. When they shed their old fur, new fur grows in its place. This process is called **moulting**. Most pinnipeds moult once a year to keep their coats healthy. They stay out of the cold water until their new fur has grown.

Did You Know?

It takes a fur seal three years to shed its thick coat of fur. It keeps some old fur for warmth while its new fur grows. There are nearly 50,000 hairs in every square centimetre of its fur!

Adult male

Young seal

Newborn pup

A family of elephant seals. The pup will shed the black fur it was born with after it is weaned.

Elephant seal shedding its old fur

Some pinnipeds, such as elephant seals, shed their fur quickly and in patches. They find a safe place to come ashore, called a **haul-out**, then lose all of their fur over a one-month period. This is called a 'catastrophic' moult because it happens suddenly and obviously. It sounds painful, but it's not.

A pup's first coat of fur is called **lanugo**. It's soft and fine. Harbour seals shed their lanugo while they are inside their mothers. They are born with a warm adult coat. Elephant seals are born with black lanugo, which they shed for a coat of silvery-grey adult fur.

How far do pinnipeds travel?

Some pinnipeds, such as northern fur seals, harp seals and walruses, **migrate**. This means that they swim long distances every year to and from their breeding and feeding grounds. Northern elephant seals make the longest journeys. Each year they swim from breeding grounds in Mexico and California to feeding grounds in the northern Pacific and Alaska, and back again.

Did You Know?

Male and female northern elephant seals have separate feeding grounds. Scientists are not sure why. Every year, males swim about 21,000 km and females swim 18,000 km.

Migratory pinnipeds return to the same breeding and feeding grounds every year. How they find their way is a mystery. They seem to have an inbuilt 'body compass' which points the way. But water and wind currents, and the taste and temperature of the sea probably guide them too.

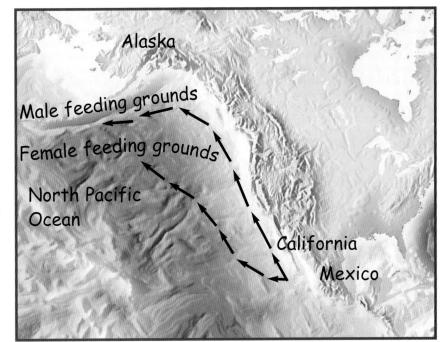

Migration route of northern elephant seals

Do all pinnipeds migrate?

Not all pinnipeds are migratory. Harbour seals, leopard seals, grey seals and many sea lion species spend all their lives within the same area.

Northern elephant seals spend most of their lives at sea.

Why do pinnipeds sing?

Pinnipeds make a range of sounds, both under the water and on land. Some sounds are threat calls, telling others to stay away, especially in the breeding season. Some are warning calls, indicating that danger is near. Weddell seals and walruses make various kinds of grunts, snorts, whines, yelps and barks. Sometimes these noises sound a little like singing.

Each colony of northern elephant seals has its own **dialect** or range of sounds.

Did You Know?

A male elephant seal's nose looks like a short trunk, which is how this pinniped got its name. In the breeding season, it blows down its nose, making noises to keep other males away.

A male walrus can sing for two or three minutes at a time. It has a range of deep notes and high whistles and makes clicks with its teeth. It also slaps its throat pouch with its flippers to make loud noises.

A California sea lion barking

Are pinnipeds in danger?

Because of **global warming**, some pinnipeds, such as those in the Arctic and Antarctic, are in danger. The temperature of some oceans is increasing – which can kill the small sea animals that pinnipeds feed on. Some pinnipeds are also threatened by pollution and hunting.

Pinnipeds have been hunted for thousands of years. They have been taken in huge numbers for their blubber, fur and meat. Some, such as the Japanese sea lion, were hunted to **extinction**. Today, countries that hunt seals are only allowed to catch a certain number of seals each year.

The Hawaiian monk seal is an **endangered** species.

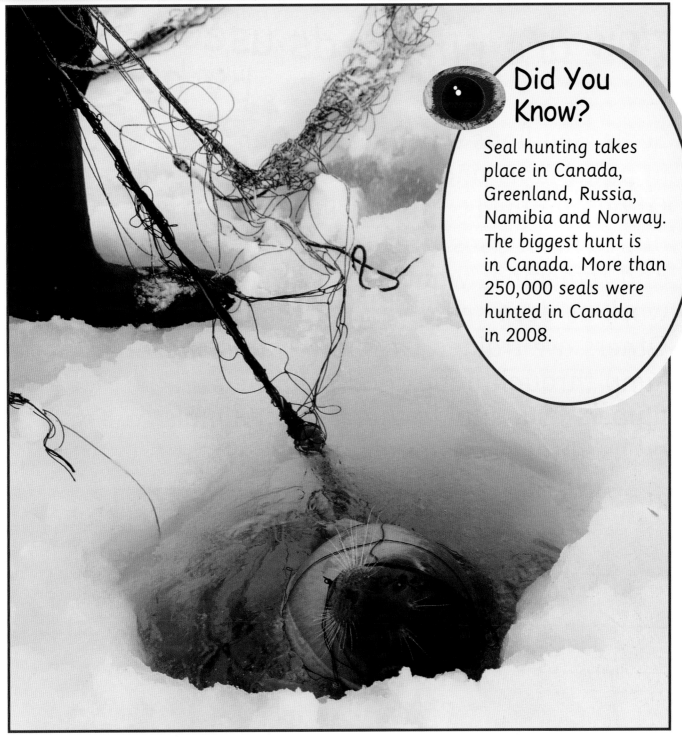

A hunter captures a seal in the Arctic.

Hawaiian monk seals (about 1,200 left) and Mediterranean monk seals (about 400 left) are the pinnipeds most at risk because there are so few of them. Special laws now protect them from harm.

The Caribbean monk seal lived in the Caribbean Sea. The last ones were seen in 1952, near Jamaica. Despite many searches, none have been seen since, and in 1996 the species was declared extinct.

How are pinnipeds used by humans?

Seals, sea lions and walruses can be seen in aquariums and zoos around the world. Of all pinnipeds, it is sea lions that are put to most uses. They are easy to train and remember what they learn. Some work as deep-sea divers for the military. Others are trained as 'show animals' to jump through hoops and clap their flippers. But should these wild animals be used for entertainment?

Captive sea lions being used as show animals in a zoo

A sea lion attaches a line to a lost missile on the seabed.

Why does the military use sea lions?

In the USA, the Navy Marine Mammal Program trains sea lions to search for underwater objects, such as mines (hidden bombs) and lost items. Sea lions can be better at this work than human divers. They can swim to the seabed more quickly than humans, and can return to the surface faster. Video cameras are attached to the animals, and their progress is watched by their trainers on board a ship.

Did You Know?

A harbour seal called Hoover could imitate human speech. He lived at the New England Aquarium, Massachusetts, USA, in the 1970s. Hoover could make sounds that sounded like 'Hello', 'How are you?' and 'Get out of here!'

Pinnipeds around the world

Pinnipeds are found in every ocean and in many seas. Some are found in very few places. For example, the Baikal seal lives only in Lake Baikal, Russia, and the Galápagos fur seal is only found on the Galápagos Islands.

Pacific walrus

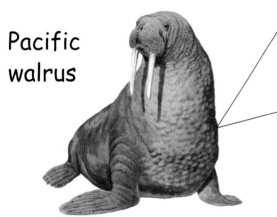

The Pacific walrus is found in the North Pacific Ocean and in the Arctic region. It mainly eats shellfish, and a hungry adult can eat 6,000 in one meal!

Galápagos fur seal

NORTH AMERICA

Atlantic Ocean

Pacific Ocean

Galápagos Islands

SOUTH AMERICA

South American sea lion

Baikal seal

The northern fur seal lives in the North Pacific Ocean, from the Bering Sea in the east to Japan in the west. It lives on fish and squid.

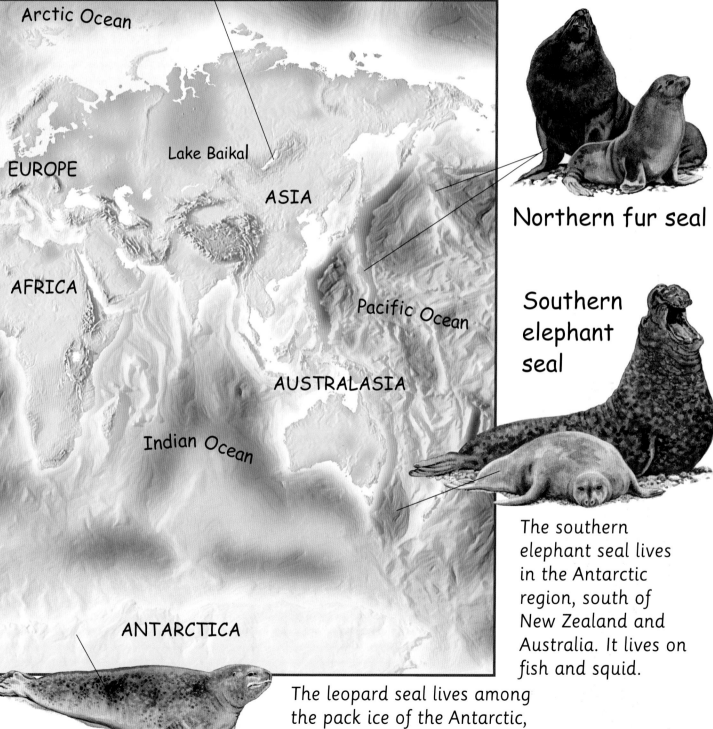

Arctic Ocean

EUROPE

Lake Baikal

ASIA

AFRICA

Pacific Ocean

AUSTRALASIA

Indian Ocean

ANTARCTICA

Northern fur seal

Southern elephant seal

The southern elephant seal lives in the Antarctic region, south of New Zealand and Australia. It lives on fish and squid.

Leopard seal

The leopard seal lives among the pack ice of the Antarctic, where it lives on krill, squid, fish and penguins.

Pinniped facts

The average cruising speeds of some pinnipeds are:
• walrus: 9 kph
• sea lion: 17 kph
• fur seal: 29 kph

As much as half a pinniped's body weight can be blubber.

An elephant seal has been found with 35 kg of gastroliths in its stomach.

Some seals can sleep underwater. Elephant seals can sleep deep underwater. Others, such as the harbour seal, sleep with only their heads showing above the water. Male walruses sleep on the water surface – they inflate their throat pouches to keep them afloat.

Inuit hunters in the Arctic listen for bearded seals under the ice. They put a kayak paddle in the water and put the handle end to their ear. The paddle picks up the sounds of the seals.

The sensitive whiskers on a pinniped's snout can detect movements nearby. In murky water, this is how pinnipeds detect their prey. A walrus has about 700 whiskers.

Pinnipeds have been seen 'playing' with fish. A California sea lion will catch a fish, then toss it into the air several times. When the sea lion loses interest it leaves the fish, and swims away without eating it.

The Baikal seal, found only in Lake Baikal, Russia, and the Caspian seal from the Caspian Sea in Asia are the world's most isolated pinnipeds.

The Baikal seal is unusual because it spends all its life living in freshwater, not in salty seawater.

The average length of walrus tusks is about 35 cm, but they can grow three times as long!

Pinniped mothers have one baby at a time. The milk they feed to their babies contains up to 50 per cent fat.

Glossary

beaching When a whale becomes stranded on a beach.

blubber The thick layer of fat just under the skin.

bull An adult male.

canine tooth Pointed tooth for tearing food.

carnivore An animal that eats other animals as its main food source.

colony A large group of animals of the same species that live together.

cow An adult female.

dialect A distinct set of sounds.

endangered Few in number and at risk of dying out.

extinction The death of the last animal of a particular species.

gastroliths Stones in animals' stomachs which help to digest food.

global warming The gradual warming of the planet.

haul-out A spot where pinnipeds come ashore.

krill Small, shrimp-like sea creatures.

lanugo Fur that some mammals are born with.

mammal An animal that is born alive and then fed by its mother's milk.

migrate To travel between breeding and feeding places at certain times of the year.

moulting Shedding old fur, skin and hair. In pinnipeds, moulting can be gradual (fur seals) or sudden (elephant seals).

odobenid (say: o-do-BEN-id) A kind of pinniped. The walrus is the only member of this family.

otariid (say: o-TAR-e-id) A kind of pinniped, also known as an eared seal.

It has ear flaps on the outside of its body.

phocid (say: FO-sid) A kind of pinniped, also known as a true seal or earless seal. It does not have ear flaps on the outside of its body.

predator Any animal that hunts other living creatures for food.

prey Any animal that is hunted for food.

pup A young pinniped.

rookery A colony of breeding pinnipeds.

species A group of animals that look alike, behave in the same way, and can breed together.

streamlined Shaped to move through air or water easily.

weaned Able to eat solid food instead of mothers' milk.

Index

A

Alaska 20, 21
Antarctic 4, 24, 29
Arctic 4, 15, 24, 25, 28, 29

B

Baikal seal 5, 17, 28, 29
blubber 6, 15, 24

C

California 20, 21
California sea lion 23
Canada 25
clam 10
colony 17
crabeater seals 17

E

eared seal *see* otariid
earless seal *see* phocid
endangered species 24

F

feeding 10, 16, 20, 21
fish 9, 10, 11, 29
fur 7, 15, 18–19, 24
fur seals 5, 17, 18, 20, 23, 28, 29

G

Galápagos fur seal 28
Galápagos sea lion 16
global warming 24
grey seal 17, 21

H

harp seal 20
Hawaiian monk seal 24, 25
hunting 24–25

K

killer whale 14, 15
krill 10, 29

L

lanugo 19
leopard seal 4, 6, 7, 8, 10, 21, 29
life cycle 16

M

Mexico 20, 21
migration 20–21
moulting 18–19

N

Navy Marine Mammal Program 27
northern elephant seal 20, 21, 22
northern fur seal 5, 20, 29

O

octopus 10
odobenid 4, 5
otariid 4, 5

P

Pacific ocean 21, 28, 29
Pacific walrus 5, 28
penguin 7, 8, 10, 29
phocid 4, 5
polar bear 15
predators 15
pups 16, 17, 18, 19

R

rookeries 17
Russia 5, 25, 28

S

sea cucumbers 10
sea lion 4, 5, 6, 11, 12, 16, 17, 21, 26, 27, 28
'singing' 22
South American sea lion 4, 28
southern elephant seal 5, 29
squid 9, 10, 29
swimming 6

T

training 26–27
true seal *see* phocid
tusks 5, 9

W

walrus 5, 6, 9, 10, 12, 15, 17, 20, 22, 26, 28
Weddell seal 12, 22

Bardd *ar y* bêl

Bardd
ar y bêl

Y lôn i Lyon

Llion Jones

Dylunio: Elgan Griffiths   Ffotograffiaeth: David Rawcliffe

I Euros ac Eleri
Brawd a chwaer yn y ffydd

ⓟ Llion Jones/Cyhoeddiadau Barddas ©
ⓟ Ffotograffau: David Rawcliffe/Propaganda ©
Delwedd Gareth Bale (t.34) ⓟ warpedwales.co.uk ©
Ffotograffau ychwanegol gan Llion Jones.

Argraffiad cyntaf 2016
ISBN 978-190-6396-96-1

Cyhoeddwyd gan Gyhoeddiadau Barddas.
Argraffwyd gan Y Lolfa, Talybont.
Mae'r cyhoeddwr yn cydnabod cymorth ariannol Cyngor Llyfrau Cymru.

Derbyniodd Llion Jones Ysgoloriaeth Awdur Cyhoeddedig Llenyddiaeth Cymru a gefnogir gan
Y Loteri Genedlaethol trwy Gyngor Celfyddydau Cymru er mwyn datblygu'r gyfrol hon.

DIOLCH
#TogetherStronger

Mae'n dda i minnau ddiolch ...

- I Elena Gruffudd a Chyhoeddiadau Barddas am gefnogaeth heb ei hail.
- I Elgan Griffiths am ei waith dylunio dyfeisgar.
- I David Rawcliffe (Propaganda) am ei haelioni a'i luniau trawiadol.
- I Osian Roberts am lunio'r rhagair a gosod seiliau'r freuddwyd.
- I Dylan, Nic, Seiriol, Emyr, ac yn arbennig Arwyn, o dîm *Sgorio* ac *Allez Cymru* am sawl cymwynas a hwb.
- I Rhys Ifans a Sion Jones (BBC Cymru) am ddod â chywydd 'Ewro 2016' yn fyw.
- I'm cyd-drydarwyr am eu cymdeithas.
- I'r garfan, y staff a phawb a fu'n gyfrifol am roi i ni rai o'n dyddiau dedwyddaf.

#GorauChwaraeCyd-chwarae

I gynnal
iaith
y galon,
gorau arf
ydy'r bêl
gron.

Roedd byd y bêl a byd geiriau yn ganolog i'm magwraeth ym Môn. Am yn ail ag ennill tlysau am gicio pêl ar gaeau'r ynys, fe fyddwn i hefyd yn cipio gwobrau am lefaru barddoniaeth o lwyfannau eisteddfod a chylchwyl.

Daeth amser pan fu'n rhaid cefnu ar rym y gair wrth i apêl y bêl fynd â'm holl fryd. Ond mae geiriau yn dal yn bwysig i mi yn fy ngwaith o ddydd i ddydd, ac yn y llyfr yma, mae'n braf gweld y ddau fyd yn cyd-fyw'n llawen.

Mae'r arwyddair 'Gorau chwarae cyd-chwarae' ar grysau tîm pêl-droed Cymru ers 1951, ond go brin y bu erioed yn fwy addas nag yn ystod ein hymgyrch yng nghystadleuaeth Ewro 2016. Daeth yr arwyddair i grynhoi nid yn unig y cwlwm rhwng y chwaraewyr a'i gilydd a'r cwlwm rhwng y chwaraewyr a'r tîm hyfforddi, ond hefyd y cwlwm rhwng y tîm a'r cefnogwyr. Roedd pob un gân, baner a thrydariad yn rhan o don fawr o falchder yn llwyddiant y tîm cenedlaethol, ac roedd pob un ohonom yn tynnu ar yr egni hwnnw.

Mae'r gyfrol hon yn rhoi cyfnod rhyfeddol yn hanes pêl-droed Cymru ar gof a chadw, a hynny ar odl a chynghanedd. Rwy'n gwybod y cewch fodd i fyw yn aildroedio'r lôn i Lyon.

OSIAN ROBERTS

Y daith i Ffrainc

Andorra 1 – 2 Cymru
9 Medi 2014
Andorra la Vella

Ar gae plastig mae'n ddigon
rhoi'r bêl i Bale yn y bôn.

Awn o dir gwael Andorra,
2 i 1, mae'n ddigon da.

Cymru 0 – 0 Bosnia-Herzegovina
10 Hydref 2014
Caerdydd

Cymru 2 – 1 Cyprus
13 Hydref 2014
Caerdydd

O Andorra a maes pryderon
i dir glasach yr adar gleision,
o awr rhyddhad i fyw breuddwydion.

Gwlad Belg 0 – 0 Cymru
16 Tachwedd 2014
Brwsel

Rhaid ydyw byw heb y bêl
i oroesi ym Mrwsel.

Dyna gêm i'w dwyn i go',
gêm *nil-nil* i'w hanwylo.

Y mae o hyd frwydrau mwy.

Israel 0 – 3 Cymru
28 Mawrth 2015
Haifa

Aaron Ramsey rŵan yw'r amser,
un hedar union cyn daw'r hanner.

Hen drawiad ar yr awel, 'Gwerth y byd yw Gareth Bale!'

Y ddraig ar 'sgwyddau'r hogiau
ydy awen talent dau.

Cymru 1 – 0 Gwlad Belg
12 Mehefin 2015
Caerdydd

Ym Mangor heddiw'r bore,
yna'r daith i lawr i'r de,
a'r haf nesaf hwyliwn ni
i Ewrop a rhagori.

Un ias, un tîm, un noson,
un dorf yn hwylio'r un don,
un gôl i danio'r galon.

Cyprus 0 – 1 Cymru
3 Medi 2015
Nicosia

Drwy haul mis Medi a'i wres
yr awn i herio hanes.

Nerth ei ben daeth Gareth Bale
i'n gyrru tua'r gorwel.

Cymru 0 – 0 Israel
6 Medi 2015
Caerdydd

Â thân o obaith ynom
ar y Sul, daeth iasau'r siom
i oeri'r dorf yng Nghaerdydd
a rhoi i obaith hen rybudd.

Bosnia-Herzegovina 2 – 0 Cymru
10 Hydref 2015
Zenica

Cyd-chwarae nid cyd-chwerwi,
hyn a wnaeth ein hogiau ni
yn enillwyr wrth golli.

Cymru 2 – 0 Andorra
13 Hydref 2015
Caerdydd

Cawsiau'n wledd, cusanau lu,
croissants, *baguettes* yn crasu ...
nesáwn at lannau'r sianel
yn byw breuddwydion y bêl.

Dau frawd iau dan ddedfryd oes.
Heno daeth hanner einioes
o obaith yn ffaith a ffydd
hen lun yn wir lawenydd.

Gyda hon, breuddwydion ddaeth
yn wir, 'sdim pris ar hiraeth
am bêl sy'n llawn symboliaeth.

Yn yr hwyl mae rheolaeth, yn yr awch
mae trefn a disgyblaeth,
cyfaddawd o ddeuawd ddaeth
i'n harwain drwy bartneriaeth.

#AshleyWilliams

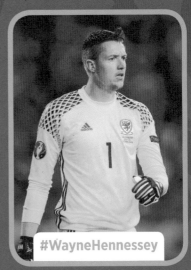

#WayneHennessey

Hwn ein llais, ein nerth a'n llyw,
hwn gadarn, ein craig ydyw.

Yn Wayne y mae'r fam ynys
a'i hunan-gred dan ei grys.

#ChrisGunter

#BenDavies

Yn y drin pan beidia'r haf,
Gunter fydd yno gyntaf.

Hen ben ffres ei wyneb yw,
dibynadwy ben ydyw.

#JamesChester

#NeilTaylor

Yn y cefn mae'i chwarae cŵl
yn troi heibio pob trwbwl.

Ag ynni ym mhob gennyn
wyt Walia ac India'n un.

#JamesCollins

#JoeAllen

O roi siawns i'r cawr sinsur
daw i'r maes a sodro'r mur.

Cael lle gwag, rhoi pas agos,
Pirlo sir Benfro heb os
yw arwr twtia'r Ewros.

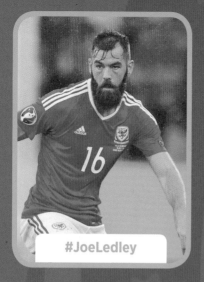

#JoeLedley

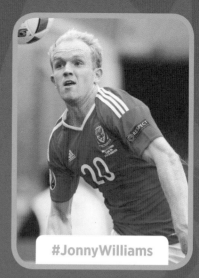

#JonnyWilliams

Pan ddaw 'na siawns i ddawnsio
a'r locsyn gael relacsio,
lej yw hwn, does neb fel Joe.

Y penfelyn llawn ynni
dyna'n Joniesta ni.

#AndyKing

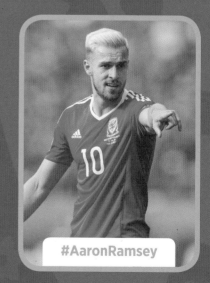

#AaronRamsey

Y mae'r brenin gwerinol
yn cynnig drwy'r tir canol
dwy lath o lafur di-lol.

O flwch i flwch, 'sneb fel hwn,
mae ansawdd tri dimensiwn
i'r dyn creu a'r doniau crwn.

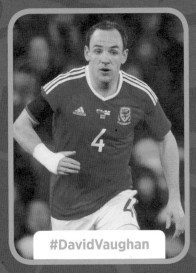

#DavidVaughan

Fy olwyn sbâr o arwr,
Pele Abergele yw'r gŵr.

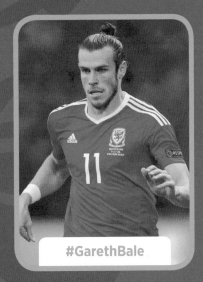

#GarethBale

Ar ei grys mae'r ddraig a rydd
i hwn ei sêl a'i danwydd.

#SamVokes

Pan welaf Sam yn llamu,
yn ôl yr wy'n anelu
i Lille yr atgofion lu.

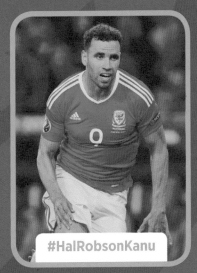

#HalRobsonKanu

Dim Hal, dim hwyl, dim heulwen,
dim rhyfelgri i godi gwên.

Paratoi i'r parti wyf

Cymru 1 – 1 Gogledd Iwerddon
23 Mawrth 2016
Caerdydd

Ar y daith draw i Bordeaux,
fan hyn yw'n hafan heno,
hon yw adeg dywedyd
au revoir tan yr haf hud.

#MarsBelieve
Dyma siocled rwy'n credu
na ddaw eto o Tesco i'r tŷ.

#Pacio
Y rhain yw lifrai parhad,
hen grysau ein goroesiad.

#Subbuteo
I'th fyd o rithiau fideo diramant,
dyro rym Subbuteo,
mae estyn fflic i gicio
ar y cae yn porthi'r co'.

#10UchafFIFA
Darlledwch drwy'r holl ludw
ein camp ni nid eu camp nhw
a rhowch, wir haeddiant yr haf,
i gochion y 10 uchaf.

#RhedegIParis
Er rhedeg drwy'r 80au,
pŵer y riff sy'n parhau
a'r ha' hwn fe awn ar ras
a dilyn y Candelas
i Baris ag un bwriad,
un gôl yw, cefnogi'n gwlad.

#GwarchodYBale
I'w gynnal ef rhag anhap,
Bale a rown mewn *bubble wrap*.

#CwpanYPencampwyr

Dos Bale, rhag y bêl yn bell,
na risgia draw o'r asgell,
ar y fainc mae lle braf iawn
i roddi gŵr amryddawn.

Panini Ddoe a Heddiw
Dwyn yn ôl ein doeau ni
wna enw gwâr Panini,
y rhain yw'r llyfrau hanes
gorau oll; ynddynt mae gwres
twrnameintiau caeau'r co'
a'r oed pan oedd pêl-droedio
yn amen ar bob munud
i un yn byw i gwpan byd.

Dymhorau'n iau, roeddwn i
yn caru'r llyfr sticeri,
hudol oedd ei hyd a'i led,
pris pecyn oedd pres poced;
yn llanc, fe dalwn â llog
i gael un o'r rhai sgleiniog,
ias o amlen byd symlach,
aur y byd mewn sticer bach.

Â sypyn mawr i'w swopio
tua'r iard yr awn bob tro,
roedd *got, haven't got* yn gân
ar gyfer y fro gyfan,
ac ym marchnad anwadal
y dwylo chwim doedd dim dal
ai digon Rainer Bonhof
yn y sêl am Dino Zoff?

Y mae'r enwau mawr yno
yng nghyfri sticeri'r co',
yn creu tîm, mae Socrates,
Tardelli, tri Ardiles,
Villa, Rossi a Fillol,
Hans Krankl, Mario Kempes, Krol;
gwelaf urddas mwstashys
a graen y pyrm *Three Degrees*.

Ond llwm oedd fy albwm i
heb Yorath, Flynn a Berry,
arwyr heb le'n yr oriel,
arwyr balch byd Cymru'r bêl,
arwyr hud ym more oes
a daniodd freuddwyd einioes
am ran i Gymru ennyd
greu â'r bêl ar gaeau'r byd.

Dwyn i go' i gadw'n gall
yw siarad am oes arall,
ond yma 'Ngwynedd heddiw
un ifanc wyf yn y ciw
yn rhannu hen gyfrinach
wrth estyn am becyn bach
sy'n dwyn ias ein doeau ni
a ninnau'n wlad Panini.

Y daith drwy Ffrainc

#MurCochBordeaux

Yn Bordeaux mae asbri'r dydd
yn lluniau ein llawenydd,
ar gyfandir ein miri,
fan hyn y mae'n gwladfa ni.

Cymru 2 - 1 Slovakia
11 Mehefin 2016
Bordeaux

Hwn yw'n dydd, bu oes gron yn dod, ein hawr
yn yr haul; daeth cyfnod
i ben, mae'r freuddwyd yn bod
heddiw ar faes rhyfeddod.

LES GROUPES

#DrannoethYFfair
Bore da iawn o Bordeaux,
y gwir sydd wedi gwawrio.

#HunlunBordeaux
Wele lun o ddau lej
yn sefyll gyda Savage.

Lloegr 2 - 1 Cymru
16 Mehefin 2016
Lens

I be rown hel i'r gelyn? Mae gennym
ganwaith gwell bathodyn,
baner, anthem ac emyn
na rhai gŵyr y lifrai gwyn.

Rwsia 0 - 3 Cymru
20 Mehefin 2016
Toulouse

O law di-dor y bore
ar Ryanair awn drwy'r ne'
i Toulouse, tua haul ha',
i anwesu'r her nesa'.

Os taw brau yw dy dablau di o hyd,
na hidia eleni,
y mae rhai na chymer hi
dair eiliad i'w meistroli.

GRŴP B	CH	E	CY	C	G+	G-	+/-	PT
CYMRU	3	2	0	1	6	3	3	6
LLOEGR	3	1	2	0	3	2	1	5
SLOFACIA	3	1	1	1	3	3	0	4
RWSIA	3	0	1	2	2	6	-4	1

UEFA EURO 2016

Yn ne Ffrainc mae cyffro'r ha'
yn dal i'r rowndiau ola'.

Cymru 1 - 0 Gogledd Iwerddon
25 Mehefin 2016
Paris

Rhown ein oll rhag llithro i'r nos,
yn Ewrop mynnwn aros.

Y mae *own goal* McAuley
yn hen hen ddigon i ni,
awn i Lille yng nghanol haf
a thalwrn yr wyth olaf.

Lloegr 1 - 2 Gwlad yr Iâ
26 Mehefin 2016
Nice

Aeth haf eu goruchafiaeth
yn hydref ymerodraeth
a'u Brexit yn exit aeth.

Cawr ar gae â'i chwarae chwim, yna tad yn anad dim.

Cymru 3 - 1 Gwlad Belg
1 Gorffennaf 2016
Lille Métropole

Morio'r ŷm yn nhymor ha'
alawon HALeliwia.

Drwy falchder y chwarteri
o Lille nawr ymlaen â ni
i Lyon yn galon i gyd,
parhawn i gipio'r ennyd.

Heno yn Lille ymhlith y gwehilion
wele hanesydd, Llywydd a Llion.

Portiwgal 2 – 0 Cymru
6 Gorffennaf 2016
Lyon

Rŵan hyn, dyw mynd adre 'nôl i ni
ddim yn wir amserol
â'r awch am un daith ar ôl,
un Nirfana derfynol.

Arni hi'r awyren hon
mae lle i gymell Llion
a'i lywio tua Lyon.

Siwrne hud fu'r siwrne hon
oleuodd Lille a Lyon
ac ar daith 'mlaen o Gaerdydd
awn ni ar antur newydd.

#GôlYTwrnamaint
Un Kanu roed i'n cynnal
ar gae chwarae, fotiwch Hal!

Ewro 2016

Ger y lan mae dagrau loes,
yno, gobeithion einioes
a foddwyd, a breuddwydion
dynion da aeth dan y don.

Yn y cof, sŵn drysau'n cau
yw tristwch taro trawstiau
a llaw ffawd yn dryllio ffydd
ar gaeau'r siom dragywydd.

Hen hanes nawr yw hynny,
o hafau hesb Cymru fu
cyniwair mae cân newydd
a'r haf hwn yw Cymru Fydd.

Yn y Rhyl, Rhosneigr, Rhos,
Garnant, Bagillt a Gurnos,
Bedwas, Bala, Llanboidy,
mae Cymru'n un ynom ni.

Ag Ewrop ar y gorwel,
da yw byw ym myd y bêl,
ciliwch o dir torcalon
yn un dorf a hwylio'r don.

#Derbyniad
Tîm gwerin nid brenhiniaeth,
mur o goch rhag Cymru gaeth.

Â'r Ewros nawr ar orwel
a Ffrainc tu hwnt i ffarwél,
down o'r gogledd ddiwedd ha'
yn ysu am daith i Rwsia.